Pebble® Plus

## Places in Our Community

# Our Post Office

by Mary Meinking

PEBBLE
a capstone imprint

Pebble Plus is published by Pebble, a Capstone imprint.
1710 Roe Crest Drive, North Mankato, Minnesota 56003
www.capstonepub.com

**Library of Congress Cataloging-in-Publication data is available on the Library of Congress website.**
ISBN 978-1-9771-1264-4 (library binding)
ISBN 978-1-9771-1771-7 (paperback)
ISBN 978-1-9771-1270-5 (eBook PDF)

Summary: The post office is an important place in our community. Many community helpers work at the post office. Readers will learn about who works at a post office, what the workers do, and what makes a post office special. Simple, at-level text and vibrant photos help readers learn all about the post office.

**Editorial Credits**
Editor: Mari Schuh; Designers: Kay Fraser and Ashlee Suker; Media Researcher: Eric Gohl;
Production Specialist: Katy LaVigne

**Photo Credits**
Alamy: David R. Frazier Photolibrary, Inc., 7; iStockphoto: PeopleImages, cover; Newscom: KRT/Beth Balbierz, 11, MCT/Fred Blocher, 13, picture-alliance/dpa/Roland Weihrauch, 19, UPI/Kevin Dietsch, 9, ZUMA Press/Hans Gutknecht, 15, ZUMA Press/Paul Rodriguez, 21, ZUMA Press/Taylor Jones, 17; Shutterstock: Album No.8, 23, Alexxndr, 2 (notebooks), Anatoliy Sadovskiy, 22 (left), Arina P Habich, 2 (post office boxes), Betelgejze, 3, jooh, back cover, Ken Wolter, 5, Naeblys, 4, 6, 8, 10, 12, 14, 16, 18, 20, Quang Ho, 22 (right), Rocketclips, Inc., 1, v74, 24

## Note to Parents and Teachers

The Places in Our Community set supports national social studies standards related to people, places, and environments. This book describes and illustrates a post office and the people who work there. The images support early readers in understanding the text. The repetition of words and phrases helps early readers learn new words. This book also introduces early readers to subject-specific vocabulary words, which are defined in the Glossary section. Early readers may need assistance to read some words and to use the Table of Contents, Glossary, Read More, Internet Sites, Critical Thinking Questions, and Index sections of the book.

All internet sites appearing in back matter were available and accurate when this book was sent to press.

Printed in the United States     5571

# Table of Contents

# Let's Visit a Post Office!

Wouldn't it be fun to choose some colorful stamps? You can use them to send cards to friends. People buy stamps and send mail at a post office. Let's go!

United States
Post Office

UNITED STATES POST OFFICE

Main Post Office
Stillwater, MN

Main Post Office
Stillwater, MN

# Who Works at a Post Office?

A postal clerk stands and works
at the counter. He helps people
send out and pick up mail.
The clerk sells stamps
and mailing supplies.

A mail sorter uses a machine
to sort the mail by zip codes.
A zip code is a set of numbers.
It tells the mail carrier
where to take the mail.

A mail carrier delivers mail.
He does the same route
every day. Some mail carriers
drive a truck. Others walk
and carry a bag of mail.

UNITED STATES
POSTAL SERVICE

119

# Post Offices Are Busy Places

Trucks arrive at the post office

early in the morning.

They bring bins of mail.

Workers sort letters, magazines,

and packages.

A mail carrier takes the mail
and begins his route.
Along his route, he picks up
letters to be mailed. He brings
the letters to the post office.

People come to the post office
to mail items. They buy stamps
for sending cards and letters.
Heavy packages may need
special postage.

Some people pick up
their own mail. It is placed
in a box at the post office.
The locked box is called
a post office box.

# Working Together

Post office workers are a team.

They work together

to deliver letters and packages.

The post office serves everyone!

21

# Glossary

**bin**—a box used to store things

**deliver**—to bring something to a person or place

**magazine**—a thin book with a paper cover that is published every week or month

**package**—a box or large envelope that is sent to a person or business

**postage**—a sticker or stamp placed on a package to show someone has paid to have it mailed

**route**—the regular path a person follows to go somewhere

**zip code**—five numbers that tell post office machines to which post office a piece of mail is going

# Read More

Barger, Jeff. *Mail Carrier.* Vero Beach, FL: Rourke Educational Media, 2019.

Donner, Erica. *Post Office.* Minneapolis: Jump!, Inc., 2017.

Kenan, Tessa. *Hooray for Mail Carriers!* Minneapolis: Lerner Publications, 2018.

Murray, Julie. *The Post Office.* Minneapolis: Abdo Kids, 2017.

# Internet Sites

*American Philatelic Society: Just for Kids: Stamp Collecting*
https://classic.stamps.org/Young-Collector

*Easy Science for Kids. A Brief History of Mail and How it Works*
https://easyscienceforkids.com/all-about-mail/

*Smithsonian National Postal Museum: Games*
https://postalmuseum.si.edu/activities/games/index.html

# Critical Thinking Questions

1. Name two jobs at the post office.

2. How do machines help workers at the post office?

3. What kinds of things are delivered in the mail?

# Index